Some Days I Make Mistakes

How to Stay Calm and Cool When Your Day Is Not So Great

Kellie Doyle Bailey, MA CCC-SLP, MMT/SELI

Illustrated by **Hannah Bailey**

Some Days I Make Mistakes

Copyright © 2022 Kellie Doyle Bailey

Published by:
PESI Publishing
3839 White Ave.
Eau Claire, WI 54703

Illustrations: Hannah Bailey
Cover: Hannah Bailey
Layout: Emily Dyer

ISBN: 9781683735601 (print)
ISBN: 9781683735618 (ePUB)
ISBN: 9781683735625 (ePDF)
ISBN: 9781683735632 (KPF)

Printed in Canada

PESI Publishing
pesipublishing.com

Hi, I'm Kela, and I'm a calm, cool kid.

And most of my days I'm proud of how I did.

But then there are days when I don't feel so great,

because... some days **I MAKE MISTAKES**.

Some days I make mistakes
when I'm learning at school.

I spill all the glitter and
I use too much glue.

I forget to walk in the halls, and I run instead
because all my friends are way up ahead!

My teachers remind me.
They ask me to walk.
I feel tears in my eyes
and it's tricky to talk.

When I make a mistake,
I feel sad and alone.
When this happens at school,
I just want to go home.

Do you make mistakes?

Do you lose your cool?

Does this ever happen when you are at school?

Some days I make mistakes when I'm at home.

I forget to feed my turtles,

and I lose my dad's phone.

KELA... Have you seen my phone?!

I knock over a chair while sweeping the floor,

SLAM!

and my sisters wake up when I slam the front door.

My parents remind me.
They say, "Pay attention, please."

I feel embarrassed inside
and weak in my knees.

Do you make mistakes?

Does this happen at home?

Do mistakes make you want to be left all alone?

It's not always easy being a calm, cool kid.
When I make a mistake, I might flip my lid.

Flipping my lid means that I lose my cool.
This can happen at home, with my friends,
or at school.

Here are some things
that can happen to me.
When I flip my lid, I might
fight, run, or freeze.

My hands get sweaty;
my heart starts to pound.
It's hard to look up,
so I stare at the ground.

When I make a mistake, I feel foolish or sad,
embarrassed, confused, or just plain mad.
I wonder if people are laughing at me,
and I want to find a quiet place to be.

Do these things happen when you make a mistake?

Do you want to run and hide because you need a break?

Do you feel hot in your face or maybe feel shame?
Do you wish you could find someone else you could blame?

Maybe you feel the same way I do.
When you make a mistake, do you lose your cool?

I remember one day when I was at school,
I made another mistake. I felt like a fool!
My heart started to pound, and I felt worried inside.
I sat down in my seat, and I tried not to cry.

My teacher saw what was happening to me,
so she sat beside me and started to breathe.
She breathed in and out with her eyes softly closed.
One breath at a time, right through her nose.

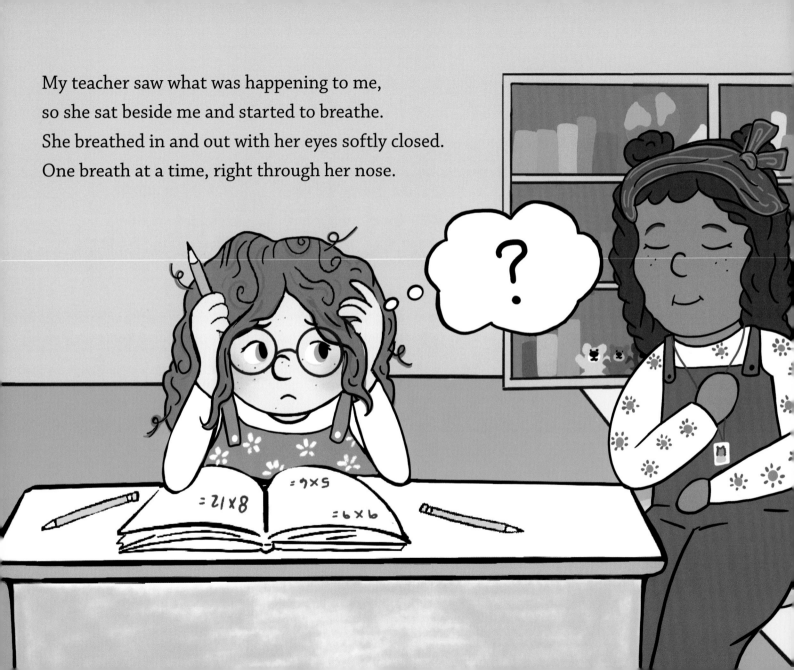

At first I thought, "That's a silly way
to deal with mistakes in school each day."
But her breathing felt calming and soothing to me,
so I started to breathe more intentionally.

I took slow, deep breaths
right through my nose.
I let my eyes soften
and then slowly close.

My heart slowed down
inside of my chest,
and my mind stopped spinning
so that I could rest.

Then, after a while, our class took a walk.
We sat in a circle, and we had a nice talk.
Our teacher showed us a mindful way
to deal with mistakes that happen each day.

She said **WE ALL MAKE MISTAKES**—both grown-ups and kids—
but we can learn how to manage without flipping our lids.
Then she shared some important things to know
so we can see our mistakes as safe ways to grow.

The first thing she said was,
"Mistakes are not bad!
We can **CHOOSE ON PURPOSE**
to feel upset or sad.

When we make a mistake,
the first thing we do
is breathe on purpose
to stay calm and cool."

"The next thing we do is get curious instead.
Mistakes can be good teachers if there's nothing to dread.
We can **SEE OUR MISTAKES AS MOMENTS TO LEARN**—
then find new solutions without shame or concern."

When we slow down our breaths during the day,
we can see our mistakes in a whole new way.
By breathing on purpose, we can be calm, cool kids.
We can solve our problems without flipping our lids.

We all make mistakes;
it's just what we do
when we're learning and growing
at home or in school.

Mistakes can be big,
or they can be small,
but no matter the size,
we can learn from them all.

Mistakes don't define us—
they help us all grow.
This is what I have learned
and what I now know.

Mistakes are not you and they are not me.
They're just how we all grow, naturally.

So let's celebrate our mistakes,
the big and the small,
and remember we're humans—
we can't do it all.

We're all in this together,
so let's do our part
and hold space for each other
with love in our hearts.

NOTE TO FAMILIES, CAREGIVERS & EDUCATORS

Thank you for reading this book with your children and for taking a moment to explore the wonderful possibilities of mistakes!

Children develop and navigate life at different rates and stages, depending upon the emotional, physical, and spiritual support they are provided along the way. This is especially true during those moments when mistakes occur.

Did you know? The most recent brain and mind science shows that by helping children learn from their mistakes, we can enhance their learning potential across their lifespan. Both effort and motivation are increased, and resilience is expanded. Wow!

Of course we want these benefits for our children, but helping them learn from mistakes isn't always easy, especially if we did not grow up receiving the message that mistakes are fantastic opportunities to learn, grow, discover, explore, and correct our errors.

Instead, we may have experienced feelings of shame, guilt, or embarrassment. Maybe we were scolded, reprimanded, given looks of disapproval, or labeled in some way when a mistake was made.

Here's some good news: It's never too late to shift our mindset about mistakes, regardless of what we've been conditioned to believe!

We can start by building our own self-awareness skills. Thinking about how we learned about mistakes and how this learning made us feel is a great place to start.

Helping our children learn to navigate mistakes both big and small—and, more importantly, the emotions that can be associated with the situations involving those mistakes—will undoubtedly have the biggest impact upon their social and emotional well-being as they develop and grow into healthy people in the world.

Even though mistakes can seem devastating to a child, it is our responsibility as adults to show that there is a positive side to getting it wrong. **Here's how:**

- Share with your child that "We all make mistakes—we are human beings, after all!"

- Share that sometimes when we make mistakes it's important to stop and notice what feelings and emotions we experience (this helps to develop a sense of self-awareness).

- Explain that we often feel guilt, shame, embarrassment, or fear when a mistake has been made, which can lead to flipping our lids and losing our cool.

- Help your child develop skills to reflect and respond, rather than simply reacting, by showing them that mistakes are opportunities to learn and grow. This helps them to develop solid self-management skills for handling challenging emotions and situations.

- Remind your child that it's okay to feel any emotion that might surface when they make a mistake, but it's not a good idea to stay stuck in a feeling if that emotion doesn't help them to feel safe, connected, and loved.

- Most mistakes are unintentional, and we can adapt and overcome these bumps in the road with loving support and guidance. Take the time to explore mistakes and the emotions that can sometimes be associated when we perceive a mistake as a moment of "failure."

- Explain that we can shift our thinking about mistakes and begin to see these situations as opportunities to learn and grow—to develop the skills of discernment, wisdom, and good judgment, which they can put into practice the next time they face a similar situation. We can turn blame and shame into curiosity and exploration to find new solutions.

Here's the most beautiful part of all:

When we teach our children that they are so much more than the sum of their mistakes, we are doing our part to change the patterns for future generations to come!

May you and your children be forever well, safe, healthy, and happy as you calm the heart, mind, and body together.

Kellie Doyle Bailey

MINDFUL PRACTICES TO HELP CHILDREN LEARN FROM MISTAKES

⭐ When your child makes a mistake, **before you talk about the "error" allow your child the space** to simply be with their emotions, regardless of what those emotions are (anger, sadness, blame, judgment, etc.).

⭐ **Regulate to help co-regulate!** One strategy is to be the "alpha breather": Stand close to your child and take slow, deep breaths in through your nose and out through your mouth, without saying a word. Simply breathe, allowing space for your child to experience your regulated calm and cool. When you notice that your child is showing signs of co-regulation (their breathing has slowed and their emotions have stabilized), simply acknowledge that "We all make mistakes some days."

⭐ **Invite your child to go for a mindful walk** outside. Notice the different colors you can see, breathe in the fresh air, and feel the ground beneath your feet. If it's nighttime, you can look up at the stars and breathe together.

⭐ Invite your child to **listen to a soothing sound,** such as water running in the faucet, for two minutes.

⭐ **Give your child a stress ball** (a small, squishy ball that fits in their hand) and show them how they can squeeze the ball while breathing in and out.

⭐ Assure your child that your care or **love for them is unconditional.**

⭐ **Name it to tame it!** Help your child identify some of the emotions that they were feeling after making the mistake. Then ask your child, "How would you rather feel?" Language is a higher-order skill, so it's best to help your child co-regulate before attempting this activity. You could also provide a feelings chart to help your child identify the emotions, or offer materials your child can use to draw how they felt and how they would rather feel.

⭐ Remind your child that not one human on planet Earth is perfect and that **mistakes are opportunities to learn and grow.**

⭐ If harm has been done to someone or something, help your child acknowledge responsibility and **repair the harm done** (with age-appropriate consequences).

⭐ Make a commitment as a family/classroom/etc. to view mistakes as opportunities to learn and grow, not as "failures," so that children won't fear making them but will rather **see mistakes as a normal part of life.**

ACKNOWLEDGMENTS

We would like to acknowledge all the educators, caregivers, and families who are working so hard to support youth. Helping children feel safe, connected, cared for, valued, seen, and represented as unique individuals while they learn and grow is a herculean effort. As educators and people who work alongside you every day—we see you and we honor you.

And to our youth—we know how hard it is to make mistakes and overcome them. Being a kid is tricky. Keep breathing. We see you and we honor you.

ABOUT THE CREATORS

KELLIE DOYLE BAILEY, MA, CCC-SLP, MMT/SELI, and **HANNAH G. BAILEY**, BA, are a mother-daughter educator creative team. Together they have brought to life the Calm Cool Kids Educate™ book series, which explores the complexities of navigating life's big emotions. Kellie is a veteran speech-language pathologist of more than 30 years and a certified mindfulness/social-emotional learning (SEL) specialist. She is the founder of Calm Cool Kids Educate™. Hannah is a middle school art educator and is pursuing her master's degree in trauma-informed education.

DEDICATION

There are so many people who deserve recognition, but for this particular book none are more deserving of the dedication than my parents, Gini and Michael Doyle. Thank you, Mom and Dad. I know that raising a strong-willed child—who wouldn't always take no for an answer and often had to learn the "hard way"—was not an easy task for either of you. Along the way we all made a few mistakes, but the one thing you never faltered at was this: Thank you for a lifetime of picking me up and dusting me off every time I fell. I'm forever grateful for your steadfast belief in me and your unconditional love, no matter how big my mistake or how hard the fall.

I love you forever and always.

—Kela-Ann